Impressionist Style

7 Original Pieces in Impressionist Style
for the Intermediate Pianist

CATHERINE ROLLIN

When I was a young student, one of the pieces that totally caught my fancy, and was a real "pupil-saver" for my teacher, was Debussy's "Le Petit Nègre." The infectious rhythms and spirit helped get me to the piano to practice. A few years later, the beauty of Debussy's "First Arabesque" was also a great inspiration and motivator. Most of the great music of Debussy and Ravel, however, is not technically or musically accessible until late high school or college. My intention in *Spotlight on Impressionist Style* was to create pieces accessible to the intermediate pianist that capture the style of the Impressionist era.

The Impressionist style has so much to do with color, imagination, rhythm and interesting pianistic devices. These are such wonderful, fun and *important* elements to explore at the piano that I hoped to give students these experiences long before they can play most of the Impressionist masterworks. It is my intent that these pieces will lead students to discover a diverse palette of colors and sounds at the piano and will show them the incredible pictures they can "paint" with their two hands and some imagination!

À votre plaisir!

Catherine Rollin

Cover art: *Boulevard des Capucines* by Claude Monet, Oil on canvas, 31 1/2 x 23 1/4 inches (80x59cm), Planet Art
Cover design: Tamara Dabney / Ted Engelbart   Music engraving: Nancy Butler

for Allegra Lilly

Iberia

Catherine Rollin

Very lively and rhythmical (Très animé et rythmé)

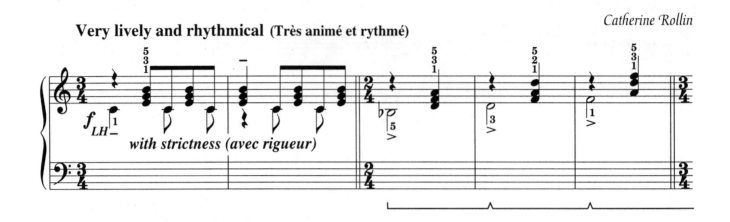

with strictness (avec rigueur)

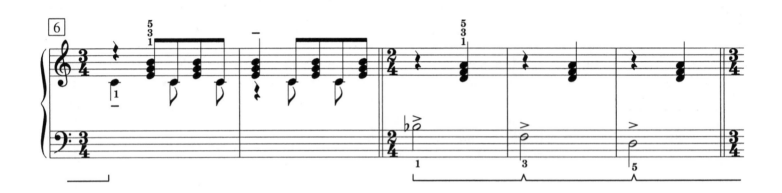

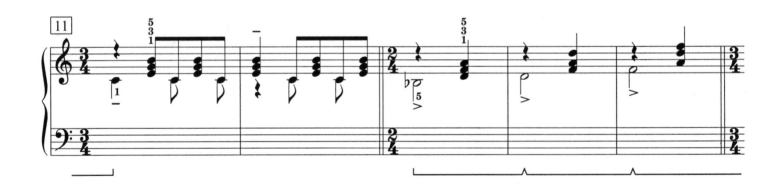

to Coda

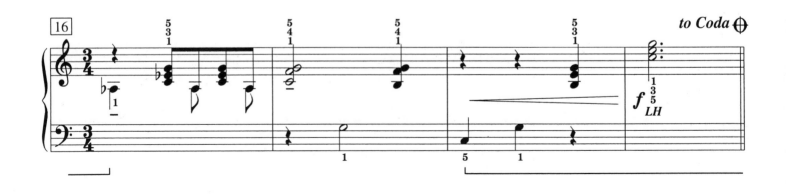

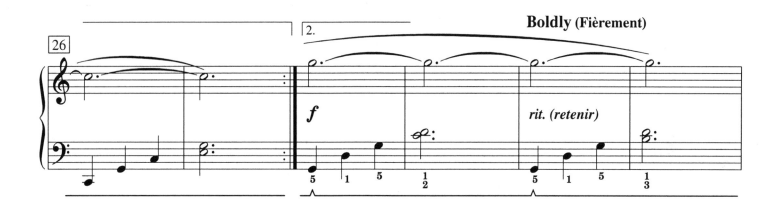
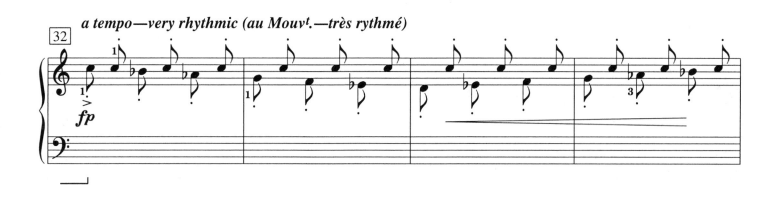
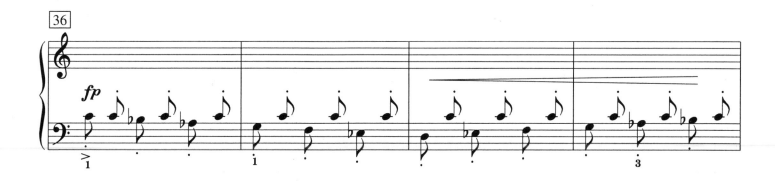

3

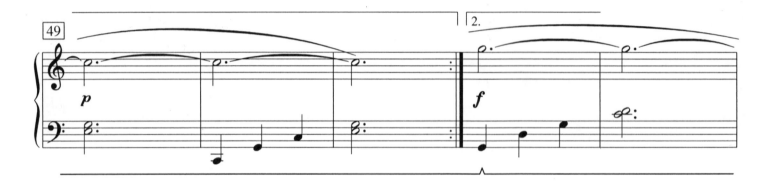

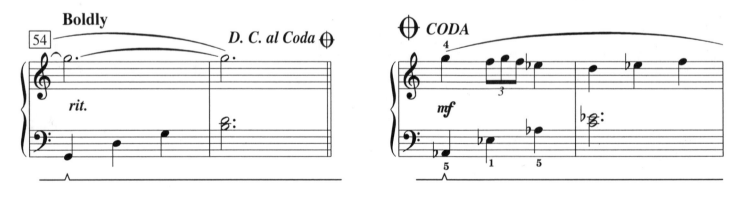

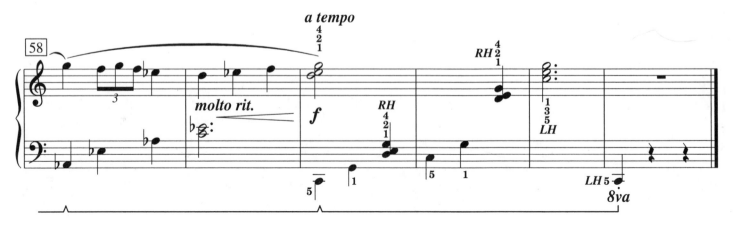

for Vera Rollin Burke

Chouchou's Cakewalk

Catherine Rollin

Very happy and rhythmical (Très joyeux et rythmé)

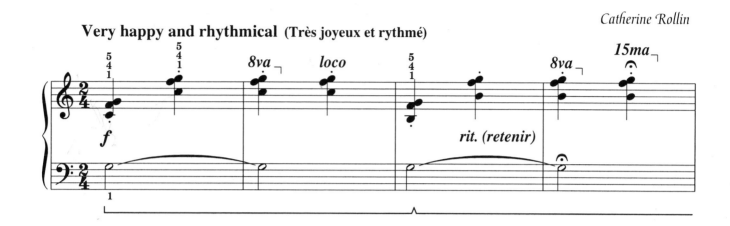

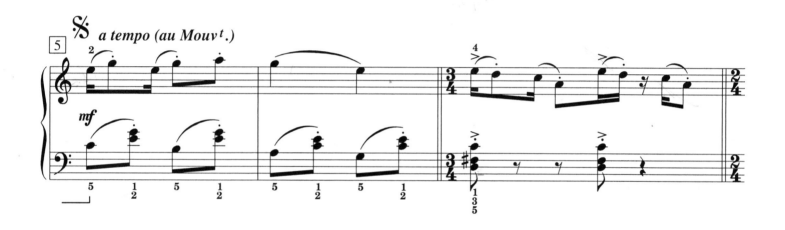

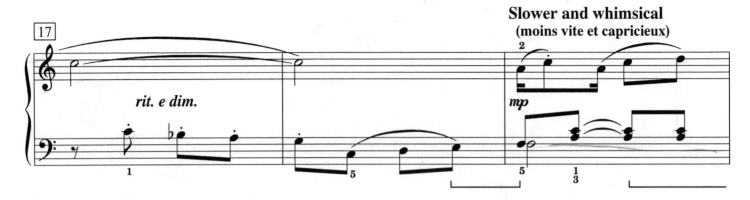

Slower and whimsical
(moins vite et capricieux)

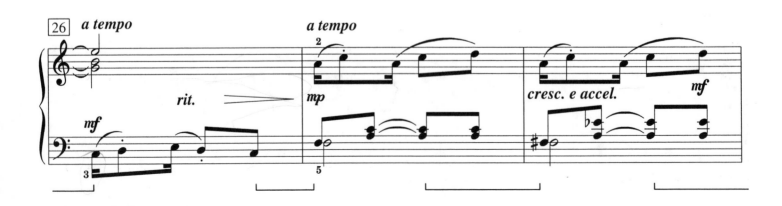

Tempo primo (Ier Mouvᵗ.)

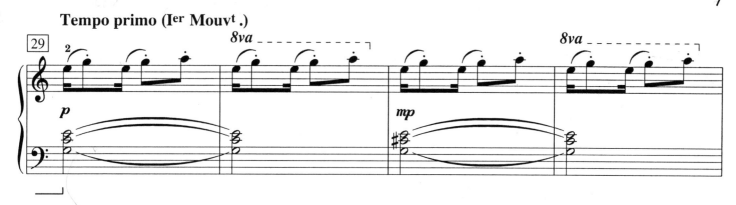

D. S.𝄋 al Coda

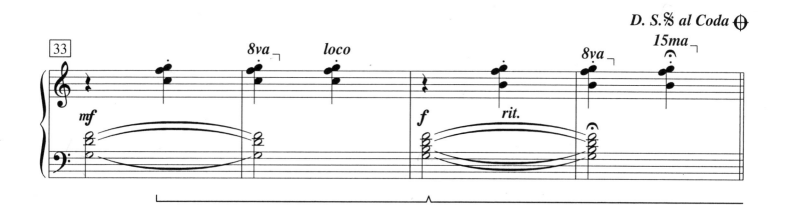

CODA

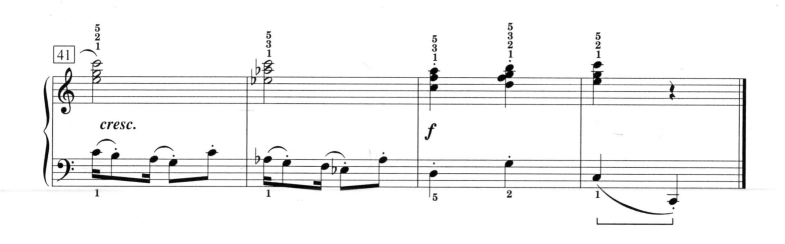

Windchimes

(Carillons dans le vent)

Catherine Rollin

Light and calm (Léger et calme)

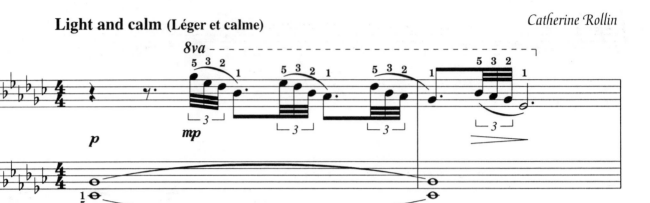

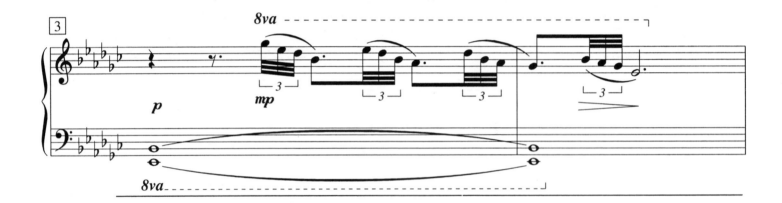

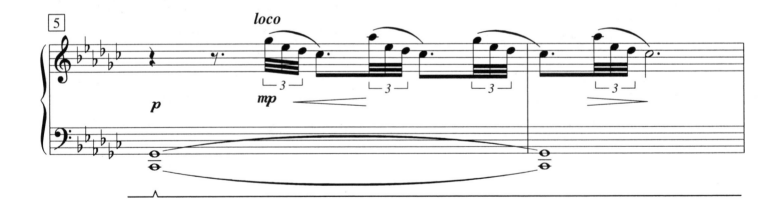

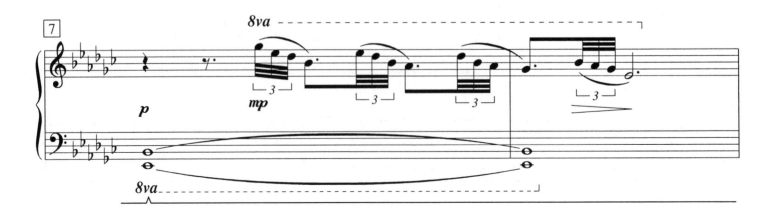

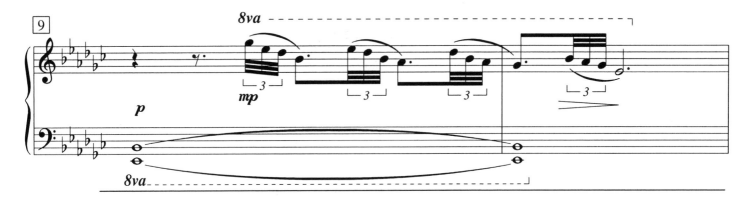

Becoming more turbulent (plus tumultueux)

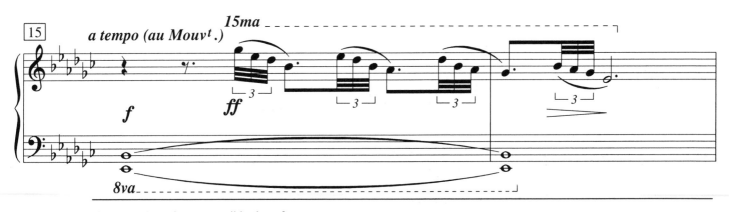

*hold back slightly and reach "a tempo" by beat 3.

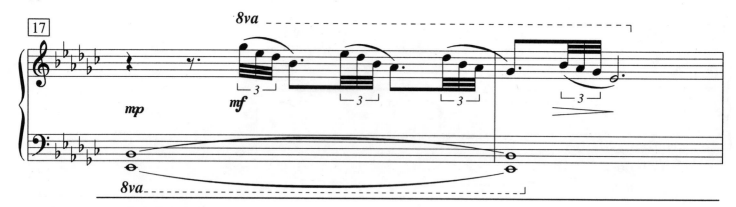

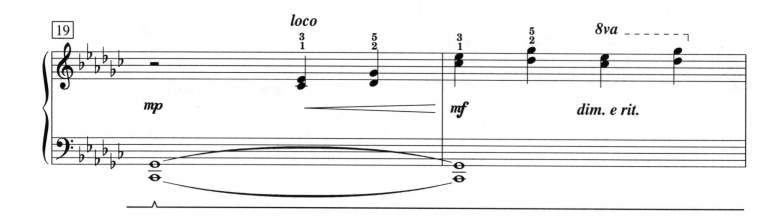

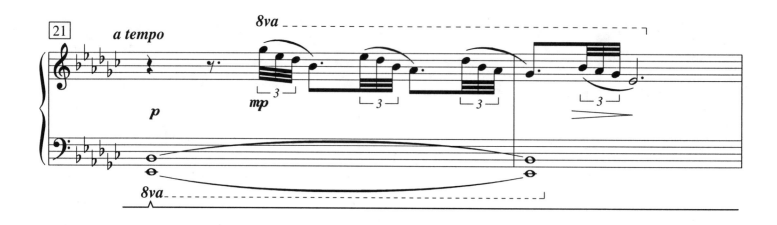

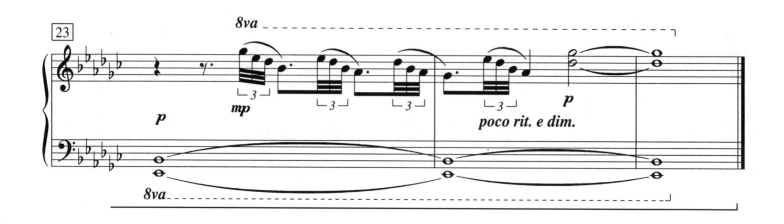

Valse Noble

Catherine Rollin

Lively and rhythmical (Animé et rythmé)

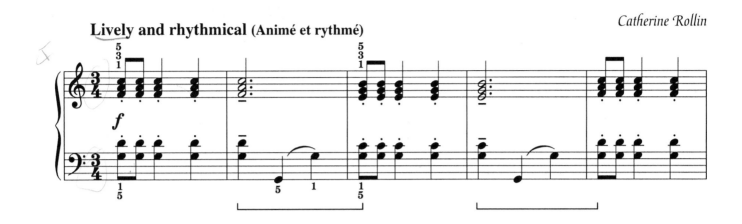

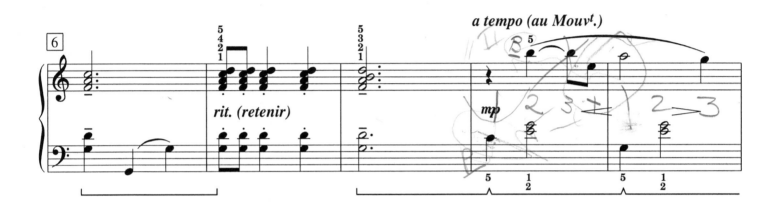

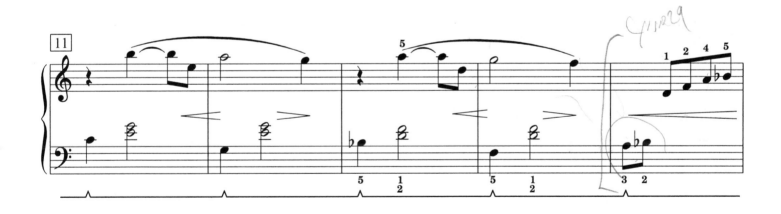

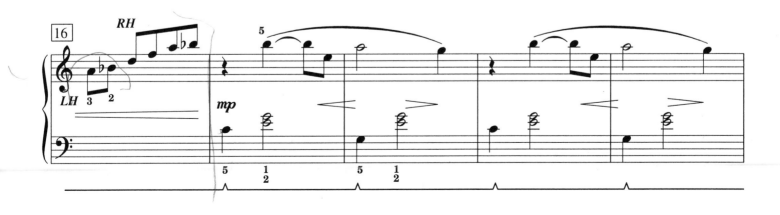

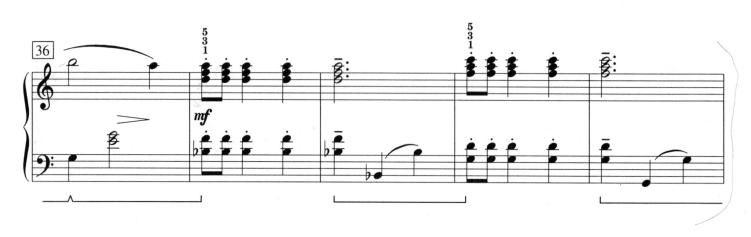

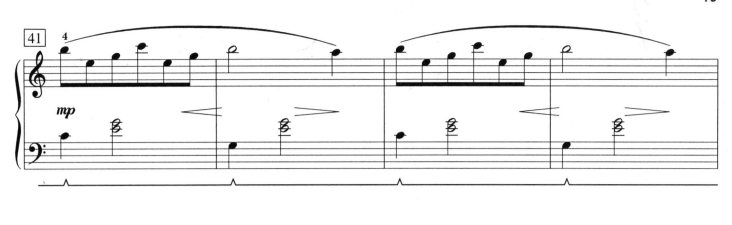

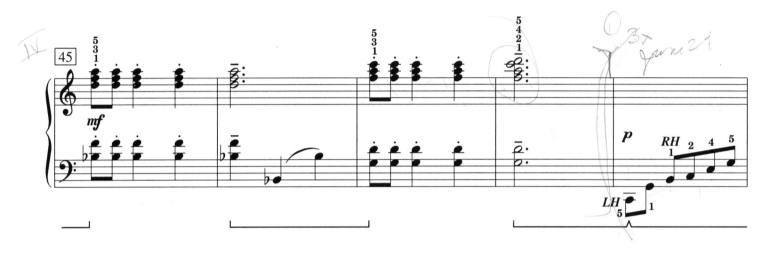

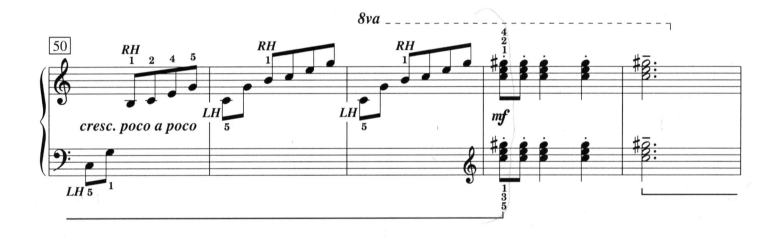

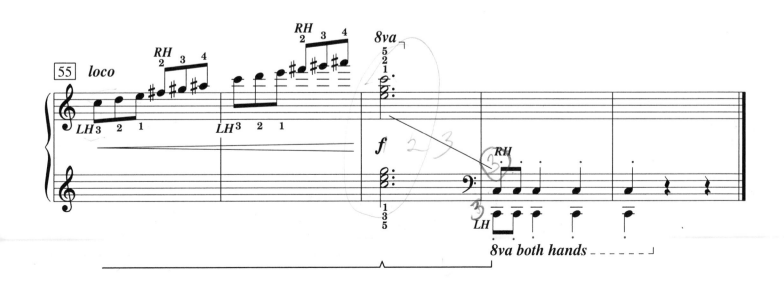

for Summer

Valse Sentimentale

Gently and with much rubato (Doucement et avec libremente)

Catherine Rollin

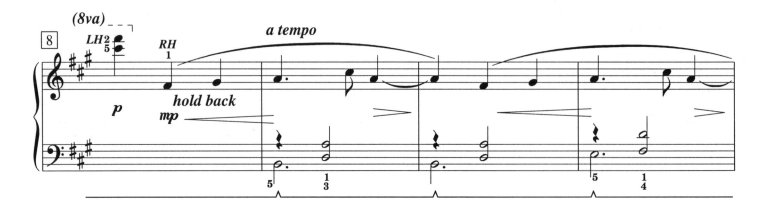

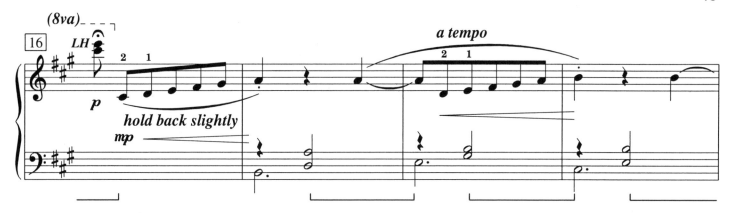

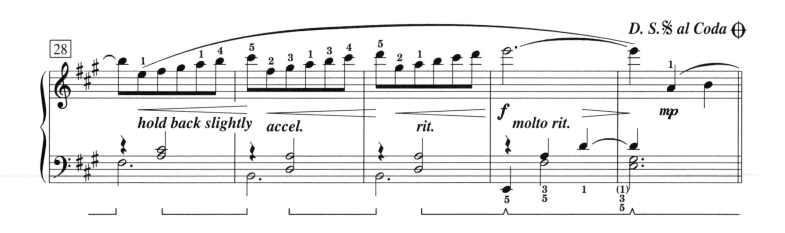

CODA

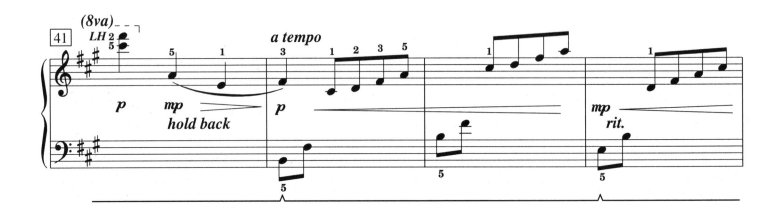

Water Lilies

(Nénuphars)

Moderate and delicately (Modérément et délicatement)

Catherine Rollin

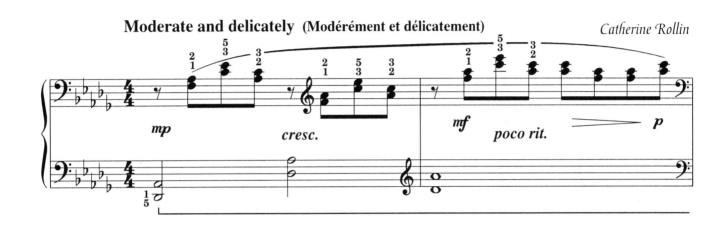

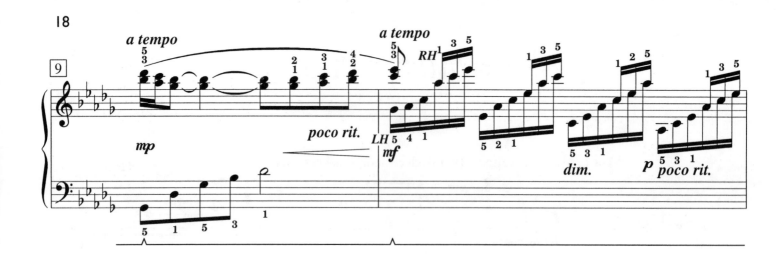

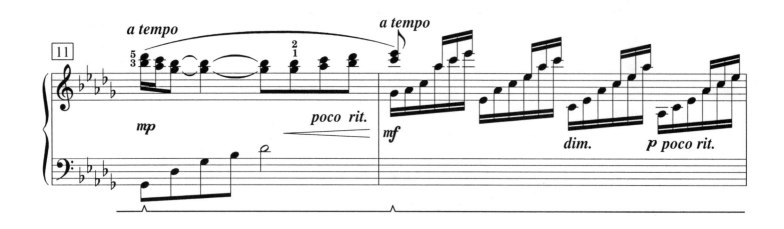

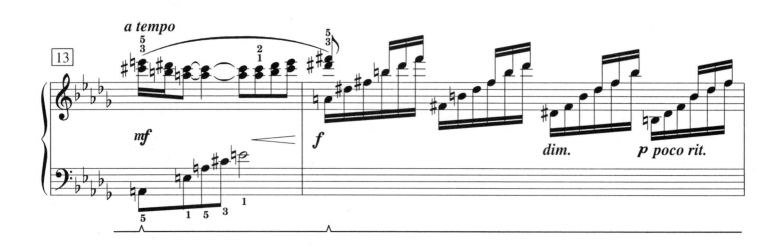

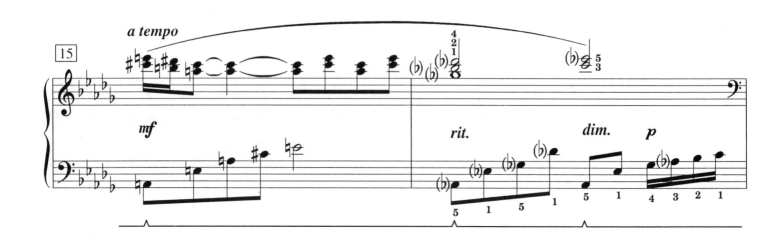

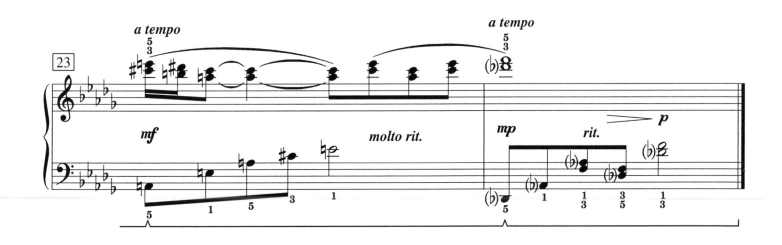

Under the Sea
(Sous la mer)

Flowing moderately (Modérément)

Catherine Rollin

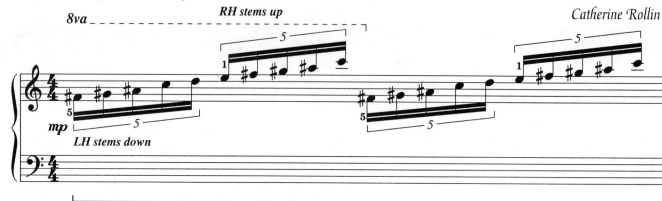

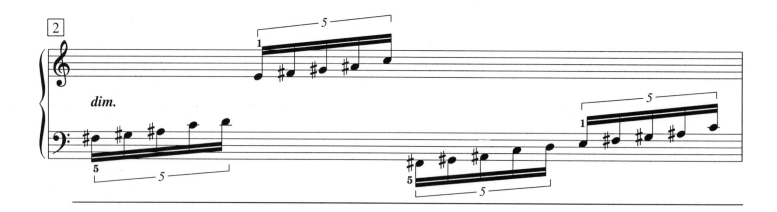

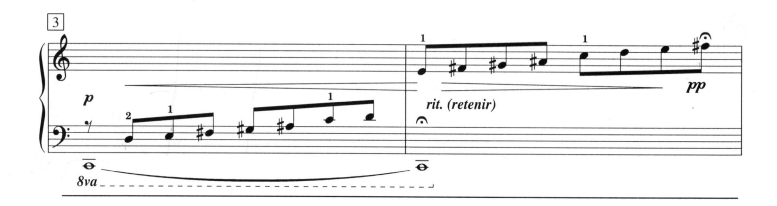

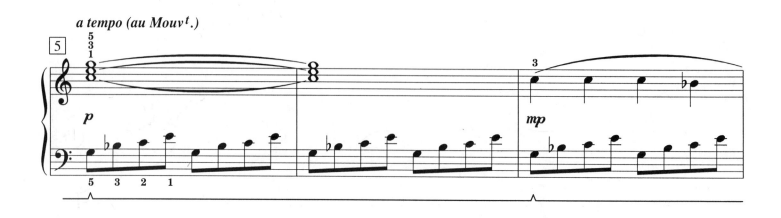

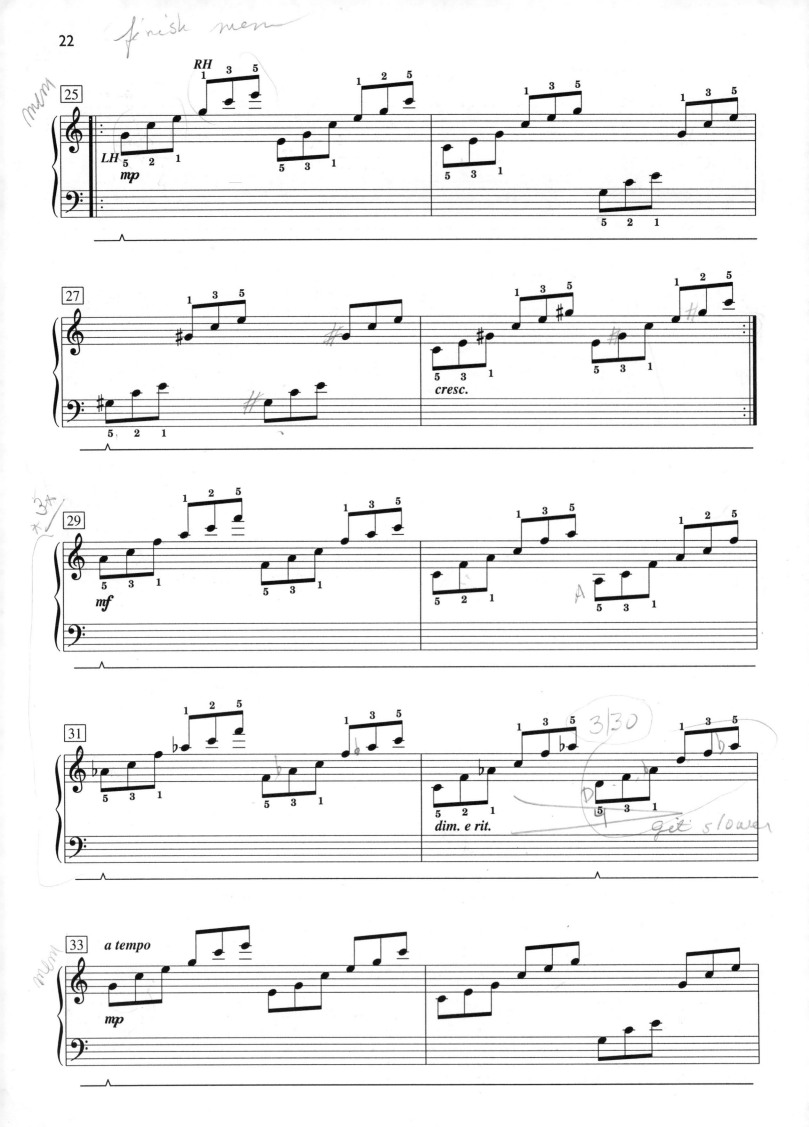

*Hold back slightly then accelerando little by little to measure 43, where the
tempo should be almost twice as fast as the starting tempo at measure 41.

Impressionism *refers to the French arts movement in the latter part of the nineteenth century and the early twentieth century. The primary composer and music innovator of this style was Claude Debussy. Maurice Ravel also contributed many major impressionistic works. Through the use of various harmonic devices (i.e., extended chords, whole-tone scales, augmented chords, bi-tonality and pentatonic scales), Debussy created music that was less oriented toward a tonal center and more concerned with creating musical imagery. Debussy experimented with many pianistic effects (i.e., alternating hands, extensive pedaling, etc.) to create a great variety of sound and musical images.*

P R O G R A M   N O T E S

Chouchou's Cakewalk is based on the cakewalk rhythm ♫♩♫ that appeared in several of Debussy's works. The cakewalk was a dance that originated in the mid-1800s by plantation slaves. Its syncopated melodies against a strict left hand were a precursor to ragtime. Chouchou was the affectionate nickname of Debussy's daughter. She was a source of inspiration for many of Debussy's playful works.

Iberia is influenced by the exuberance of Spanish dance rhythms. Many of Debussy's works reflect this influence. Iberia also uses a lot of alternating hand technic, which is a prevalent device in Debussy's piano writing.

Under the Sea (Sous la mer) evokes images of the sea. Both Debussy and Ravel wrote many works influenced by water imagery. The introduction of this piece is based on a whole-tone scale. Void of half steps, whole-tone patterns are harmonically perfect to emulate the amorphous nature of water. This piece also uses augmented seventh chords (measure 5), augmented chords (measure 27) and bi-tonality (measure 41). These harmonic devices help elicit water imagery.

Valse Nobles and *Valse Sentimentale* reflect the strong influence of the waltz on the writing of both Debussy and Ravel. Sometimes it is treated adoringly and with sentiment, as in Debussy's *Valse Romantique*, and at other times it is almost mocked as the symbol of the end of an era, as in Ravel's *La Valse*. The waltzes in this collection are intended to capture both its bold drama (*Valse Noble*) and its delicate and whimsical side, which reaches expressive heights through extensive rubato in *Valse Sentimentale*. In *Valse Noble*, extended chords lend this romantic dance its impressionistic color.

Water Lilies (Nénuphars) is inspired by the art works of Claude Monet. Much of the music of the Impressionist era is intended to capture visual ideas through our aural imagination. The use of extended chords (sevenths and ninths) help create these images.

Windchimes (Carillons dans le vent) is largely based on a pentatonic scale comprised of all black keys. Both Debussy and Ravel were dedicated to introducing musical sounds and rhythms of other cultures into their music. They were influenced by the five-note pentatonic scale that was prevalent in Asian music.